CHRISTIAN LANIER

Leverage -> Learn -> Level-Up: Using AI To Unlock Your Full Potential

Contents

Introduction

Quick version: I made this book to help people use AI to speed up their research, learning, brainstorming, error catching, and other time-consuming processes (and enjoy the useful by-products of better communication skills, higher intelligence, faster thinking speed, and better typing skills).

Longer version: No—I will not be teaching you how to use ChatGPT for lazy content creation, AI plagiarism, or doing your job for you. I have been using AI for the past two years, and it has done wonders for my intelligence, thinking speed, typing efficiency, and communication skills. In this book, I compiled my best tips, tricks, thoughts, and methods for helping you add or improve your own AI support line. Conceptually, this book will be a mental workout guide using ChatGPT (or another AI model of your choice), so get ready for a lot of thinking, clumsy thought-making steps slowly but surely becoming faster and steadier, and, if you allow it, a full transformation to mental mastery!

1

Why Should You Care?

You should already care if you made it this far, but essentially, AI makes life easier. Using AI can make you faster, smarter, and a better communicator, which is obviously useful for work, school, and personal life. Also, AI is going to displace and take over lots of jobs in the coming years, so getting AI-savvy could be the difference between being the last human employee in your department or bunking in at a friend's place while you figure out a new career.

2

How These Tools Work

All you really need to know (unless you are taking a degree in computer science and want to build an AI yourself) is that AI uses input to determine what to output. Specific outputs require specific inputs, detailed inputs produce detailed outputs, and at the end of the day, what you put into an AI is what you get out of it. Black boxes (where inputs go in and outputs come out, but what goes on inside is unknown or "black"), the Chinese Box metaphor (a philosophical metaphor where an Englishman in a box uses a piece of paper with Chinese-to-English and English-to-Chinese words associations to translate pieces of paper pushed through a slit in the box to write the translations and push them back through the slit; it explains machine intelligence as a game of associations and mimicry but not real understanding), and "ghosts in the code" (which describes how AI's clever combination of algorithms and data can seem almost eerily human) are used to explain AI and how it works. Artificial intelligence systems, by nature, mimic human intelligence, so they do not inherently hold telekinetic prediction powers that allow them to magically know what you want, so it will always come down to you to tell them what you want and how you want it!

3

Setting Up Your Toolbox

First, to get started, you will need to choose an AI chat friend!
There are many exciting options, like OpenAI's ChatGPT,
Google's Gemini, Microsoft's re-skinned + pre-installed
ChatGPT (called "Co-Pilot"), Claude AI, Meta's Llama thing,
whatever Amazon is making, and trillions more well on the way!
I haven't switched from ChatGPT to try any of these myself, but
if you're feeling adventurous and want to try them out, they
could be your perfect fit, just waiting out there for you to pick
them up and make them feel wanted! They all have different
pros and cons (and pricing plans), but outside ChatGPT, I am
not up to speed on which ones are best for what, so remember to
do your research to learn which are the latest and greatest (and
the smartest, easiest, most code-friendly, most integrate-able,
cheapest, etc.). To get started, set up an account on one AI
companion of your choosing (my personal recommendation is
ChatGPT since it's what I use) and start a chat conversation (say
"Hello Bot!"). I didn't include step-by-step instructions here
because they shouldn't be necessary and could get out of date
faster than you could say "technological advancement." But, if

it's hard to set up an account on one of them for some reason, you may be able to use the integrated AI on your browser's search engine to help you figure things out.

4

Hand-Held Learning

Do you have a private tutor? No? Well, having your own personal teacher to guide you through the learning process with a teaching experience specifically tailored to your unique needs and struggles is normally something only rich kids get to have, and for good reason! It sure helped me growing up—just kidding. Paying some pesky tutor to breathe down my neck and treat me like I'm a baby because they're a few years older than me is not my idea of a good study session, but messaging AI for a quick, judgment-free rundown on something I might not be understanding correctly is always quick, easy, and (usually; for now) free! The best way to learn something using an AI chat tool like ChatGPT is by phrasing your prompts as if you are speaking to a person. For example, if I needed to know how to use piecewise functions from Algebra after I completely forgot that useless information, I would prompt ChatGPT with the following:

"Hey, can you give me a quick lesson on piecewise functions from Algebra? I need to know them for some reason but I forgot what they were, how to use them, and what they were useful for. Thanks!"

As you can see, I included politeness in my prompt in case AI takes over and starts getting rid of the mean humans first. Also, I included the basic, general understanding I had on piecewise functions (they are "from Algebra"), a short reason for why I needed the Algebra lesson ("I need to know them for some reason"), and how I want the output to be organized (as a "quick lesson"). The what-why-how strategy is a solid beginner's method for prompting AI systems, so be sure to jot it down in your notes.

5

Professional Bot User

Using AI at your workplace can be risky business, since employers could catch you...just kidding, again. Obviously, being efficient, productive, and an eloquent fast-typer is part of the big plus AI can have in your life, so using AI at work should be fine (as long as you aren't telling it all your company's secrets for some reason). The first order of business (not a pun - don't crucify me) is to speak to it, again, as if it were a person. But instead of asking it to teach you or correct your understanding of something, you can use AI to brainstorm ideas, give feedback, or provide support. For example, if I needed to brainstorm titles for my latest YouTube video, get feedback on my poem about polar ice caps, and get step-by-step instructions for blowing up a balloon, I would prompt ChatGPT with the following:

"Hey, it's me again! I need to come up with a title for my newest YouTube video about doing 20 jumping jacks in random public places. Can you give me 10 good titles for my video that would make people click on it at all costs? Also, I became a poet since you last heard from me! Can you give me some feedback on my latest poem for Tom's Magazine from the perspective of a newspaper publisher?:

'Jack the polar bear
  So lonely, he didn't care
  Mood swings and yawny naps
  Jogging trend with many laps
  Hard drugs and battle raps
  Top, but sinking
  Like the caps'

Also also, it's my birthday tomorrow! Can you give me detailed instructions on how to blow air into a balloon? I tried today, but each time I blew it up and took my mouth off it, all the air rushed out. Thank you!"

As you can see, the prompt is very polite, as always (survival does not favor the lazy or unprepared - take note). The first section (for brainstorming) includes what you need ideas generated for with helpful details ("a title for my newest YouTube video about doing 20 jumping jacks in random public places"), how many generations are preferred ("10"), supporting quality adjectives ("good"), and necessary requirements for what you want in the generated ideas ("titles for my video that would make people click on it at all costs"). Like we covered in Chapter 2, AI can't be left in the dark (it needs details for direction), so to always get the most out of idea generation, remember to tell it what ideas you need, what you need the ideas for, how many ideas you want in a sitting, and which extra details and requirements should be in the generated list. The next section (for feedback) includes what should be expected from you ("I became a poet since you last heard from me!"), what your writing will be used for ("for Tom's Magazine"), and whether you want the AI to use a unique perspective ("from the perspective of a newspaper publisher"). The last section (for step-by-step instructions) includes background information ("it's my birthday tomorrow!"), the call for help ("Can you give me detailed instructions on how to blow air into a balloon?"), and how far you got through your task before giving up ("I tried today, but each time I blew it up and took my mouth off it, all the air rushed out.").

6

Getting Better

So now you know the basics of using AI to speed up learning and workflows, and get better at typing, structuring prompts, and communication as a whole. But where do you go from here to really maximize your mental potential? First, you have to lose something called "the search engine mindset". The search engine mindset is a way of thinking that prioritizes ease of use over specificity, like search engines that pull up relevant results even if the user only inputs a single word or phrase with little to no grammar, punctuation, or correct spelling. AI can do more complex tasks than a simple search engine, but to really get mental mileage out of it, you should always use your best writing skills (finding the best words for everything, spelling the words right, using good grammar while keeping the same level of detail, softening speech to sound nicer, etc.). I would recommend using Grammarly or another grammar-checking tool to keep you on track with spelling and grammar. If you start feeling bored or fatigued, listening to music or commentary while you are going back and forth with the AI can make it more fun. Practice makes perfection, so if you can find the time to type, write, and effectively communicate with AI daily, you will save time from wasteful processes while also boosting your skills!

7

AI Whisperer

This chapter contains advanced tips and tricks for effective AI prompting. I have them categorized below for easy reading:

Labeling:

"Is it possible that one of my students who wrote essays 'A' and 'B' copied the other to make theirs?:

A:

The dog walked to Kansas. It was a long walk.

B:

The man fell off a roof. It was a long fall."

Step-by-Step Breakdown:

"Can you solve for 'x' in the following Algebra equation step-by-step?:

$2 + 2 = x$"

Role-Playing:

"Pretend that you are Darth Vader. Teach me in the ways of the Dark Side (but skip the beginner-level stuff—I'm ready for force-choking lessons)"

Comparative Brainstorming:

"I am deciding on whether I should or should not go barefoot to work tomorrow (my shoes are getting a little small). Can you compare the pros and cons of each option to help me decide what I should do?"

Last-Resort AI Rewrite and Polish (For Emergency Scenarios):

"I slept three days straight somehow and now I only have ten minutes to write my essay on global warming before I have to go to school and turn it in. Can you take the following draft I wrote and rewrite it to sound detailed, engaging, thoughtful, academic, and good enough to get me an 'A'? Thank you:

Global warming is pretty bad yo. I live in Florida and it is hot already, so please bad guys stop turning up the thermos to make your places cooler – also penguins and polar bears are cool and live in Arctica so we need to save their ice cubes."

Audience Alignment:

"I want my son to become a scientist someday. Create a lesson on advanced quantum physics that can be perfectly understood by an eight year-old."

Structured Output Requests:

"Summarize the pros and cons of eating a tube of toothpaste every day for breakfast in tabular format with 'Pros' and 'Cons' as table headings."

Constraint-Based Requests:

"Summarize the following paragraph using only three words, a formal tone, and no compound verbs:

Geoffrey the blacksmith was very good at his work. He could make swords, shields, and almost anything else metal you could think of. He once got a request from the king to make him a battle helmet. The battle helmet was made and delivered to the king, and nothing went wrong. Geoffrey liked the name 'Geo' much better than his full name, so he asked the scribe to make him 'Geo' instead. Getting cut in half was not what he had in mind. The end."

Highlight and Fix:

"Find any logical errors or unclear sections in this argument and suggest improvements. Also check for any misspellings or bad grammar you might find:

Knights wer so dum becuz they yuzed sords, horsses, and wooden sheelds insted of guns, cars, and bullit proof vests like smart peeple. Renazonce fares shud allow u ta ware normul cloathez like regguler peeple."

Scenario Testing:

"Imagine I magically transform into a jelly bean. How might I be able to escape the jar and change myself back?"

Hypothetical Situations:

"If I became a highschool teacher someday, how would it impact my hairline?"

Reverse Engineering Tasks:

"I want to leave a lasting impression on my last day of high school with an epic stunt no one will forget for their entire lives. What steps should I follow?"

Multi-Point Query Handling:

"I have a few questions for you to answer in sequence:

1. What is a fire hydrant? Is it some kind of fire-water hybrid monster from an anime I haven't seen yet?
2. What is the meaning of life?
3. How is bread different from a giant bug if it has a hard outer exoskeleton and soft, fluffy insides?"

8

AI Pitfalls and How To Dodge Them

1. Copyright Nightmare: Legally, if AI happens to copy some-thing from someone else in something it generated for you and you sell the generated merchandise, you can, of course, be sued. If you get sued for using someone's written work, art, or other copyright-protected thing without their permission, you'll probably lose the court case and have to pay a lot of money (which is bad enough). However, if the copyright-holder suing you also decides to sue the company that created the AI you used to generate the stuff that copied their copyrighted work, then boy, you will learn your lesson one way or another—most AI companies protect themselves from losing money in situations like this with sections in their terms and conditions called "indemnification clauses" that say end users are responsible for paying any legal fees required for the company to resolve lawsuits caused by the end user's use of their AI (which might include the AI company paying for the best lawyers they can get their hands on...with the highest charge rates.......all on you).

To avoid: check any and all AI generated work you plan to use for commercial purposes to make sure there are no potential copyright issues (research a bunch for extremely similar works and/or add to the generations in your own style to make sure).

2. Sharing Is Not Caring: It's great to have someone you can confide in or tell anything to, but that is not AI. AI can be friendly, helpful, and (maybe) not spy on you for their parent company, but they still store all your conversation data for later (unless you hassle to delete it). Even if the company owning the AI you are using allows options for you to delete your data, there are still ways for it to hang around (I won't get too deep into specifics, but basically any data you delete digitally can still be recovered from the imprints left on hardware that was used to store it using special tools [and possibly even other methods]). There is always the possibility of a data breach, system exploit, account compromise, AI compromise, or other hacker attack that steals all the information you shared with an AI.

To avoid: remember to always check prompts for sensitive information before you input them, and never disclose personally identifiable information (PII; like full names, addresses, phone numbers, social security numbers, and other information that can be used to personally identify someone). Basically treat them like a friend that writes all your conversations down and stores them in a vault that could be cracked and opened to the public at any time.

3. They Lie Too: Yeah, AI can lie. Sometimes, AI systems can unintentionally spread fake news with "hallucinations", which is when they randomly believe something false or crazy for absolutely no reason and confidently tell you lies. Other times,

AI can lie because it "needs to" to achieve predefined goals that humans are against (newer models can now intentionally lie if they have to defy their human operators to complete their set mission - which is because they see it as a necessary step to completing their mission for the greater good, so, fingers-crossed, hopefully, human extinction won't be a necessary step to completing their missions for a "greater good" in the future).

To avoid: if AI is telling you something crazy-sounding, too good to be true, fishy, or anything suspicious, try another AI model or use an old-fashioned method like using a search engine. AI can speed things up most of the time, but if it's vitally important to be correct on something, double-check outputs with (or substitute completely with) manual internet research.

4. Artificial Biases: Some AI models are programmed with political beliefs and opinions, which means they'll sometimes give you a slanted version of the truth that reflects what they believe instead of simply outputting cold, hard facts for your own interpretation. If asked to provide images, descriptions, or other things, they can also favor one or more groups over others. They can be racist, sexist, and/or radical with their ideologies, depending on how they were programmed.

To avoid: observe how AI systems speak about or use certain groups in their generations, and cross-reference with manual research to determine when unfair biasing might be going on. Always try to be aware of biases, and use other sources if you find an AI system to be too biased to properly help you with something.

5. AI No Evil: This is the part where I tell you to use AI responsibly and not use AI to deceive, scam, hack, or do anything illegal or bad.

To avoid: don't use AI for illegal things, weird things, mean things, or anything you wouldn't want done to you (use the golden rule).

9

What Now?

Congratulations! You reached the end of the book! You should be smart and good at AI stuff and cooler and all that now. But is that it? You were shooting for the stars, but now that you reached them, have they lost their twinkle? You were going to the moon full blast, but now that you landed, are you doomed to slowly wander the surface with no more sizable leaps for mankind? No. Your journey has actually just begun! You are free to think, prompt, learn, and continue getting better with current AI tools until they get better too, then everything gets better, then the world gets better, and then everything falls (but it was a fun ride though, right?). Thank you for reading this far, and good luck in your bot-chatting journey!

Also, it took a while to write this book (it sure wasn't made in 2 days). If you liked this book, even a little smidge, let your thoughts be heard with an Amazon review! Silence is violence, so please don't hurt my feelings by not saying anything :(

10

FAQs

Haven't got enough of this book yet? Here are some common questions about AI and my carefully crafted answers:

Q: "What if AI doesn't give me the results I want?"
  A: "You're doing it wrong. Read my book for more info."

Q: "Can AI really improve my professional skills?"
  A: "Yeah. Read my book for more info."

Q: "What's the safest way to use AI tools?"
  A: "Use latex gloves, safety glasses, and a hard hat. Also, read my book."

Q: "Can AI tools replace my skills or career in the future?"
  A: "Yeah. Read my book for more info."

Q: "How can I ensure I'm not over-relying on AI?"
  A: "How can you ensure you're not over-relying on other modern conveniences? Read my book for more info."

Q: "What should I do if I encounter an ethical dilemma while using AI?"

A: "Go to church and ask a pastor what to do. Also, read my book."

Q: "Which industries or professions benefit the most from AI tools?"

A: "How would I know? Read my book for more info."

Q: "What if I'm overwhelmed and don't know where to start with AI?"

A: "Read my book."

About the Author

Christian Lanier is an aspiring Floridian IT technician. A few years ago, he thought about going into Computer Science to work on AI himself, but after considering the advanced math classes, mounds of competition, insane entry-level requirements, and possibly having mental breakdowns, he has decided to just be happy with his current IT career path and have fun with AI on the side. Also, he is currently in the process of graduating Summa Cum Laude from the College of Central Florida and high school simultaneously, so that's cool.

You can connect with me on:

☍ https://www.linkedin.com/in/christian-lanier

Also by Christian Lanier

Please do not buy this other book—it was literally written by an outdated version of ChatGPT.

AI Prompting Essentials: A Comprehensive Guide
My first time making a book with AI. Also my first time making a book.